STECK-VAUGHN

PORTRAIT OF AMERICA

New Hampshire

Kathleen Thompson

A Turner Book

RSVP

RAINTREE
STECK-VAUGHN
PUBLISHERS

The Steck-Vaughn Company

Austin, Texas

New Hampshire

Berlin

FRANCONIA NOTCH
STATE PARK

Littleton

WHITE
MOUNTAINS

▲ Mount
Washington

Lincoln

Conway

Hanover

Franklin

Lake
Winnipesaukee

Lebanon

Laconia

Connecticut River

Merrimack River

Claremont

Rochester

CONCORD ✪

Dover

Portsmouth

Keene

Manchester

Derry

Amherst

Nashua

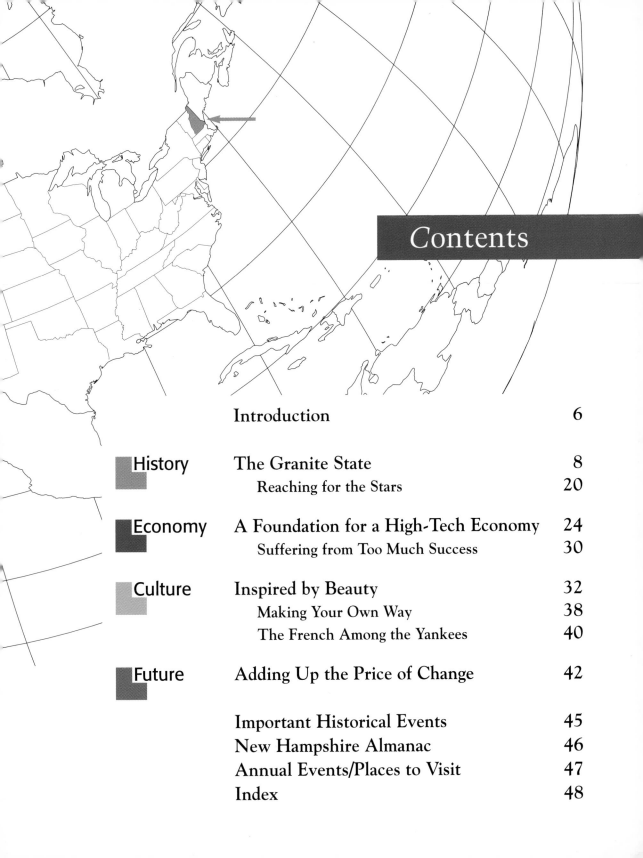

Contents

Introduction

The people of New Hampshire have a reputation for free thinking and determination. These are qualities made famous by their ancestors, the men and women who settled this beautifully rough land. New Hampshire settlers used what nature offered. They cut down trees to make room for farms and built homes and furniture from the lumber. They built stone walls with the boulders scattered across the landscape. When they couldn't move an object, they planted around it. And when the people of New Hampshire faced the decision to make their own laws, they did not hesitate. Their response is the motto of the state: "Live free or die."

New Hampshire's Mount Washington is one of the highest mountains east of the Mississippi. It is 6,288 feet tall.

New Hampshire

Monadnocks, Dover, Mount Washington

FRANKLIN PIERCE

FOURTEENTH

PRESIDENT

The Granite State

Hundreds of years ago, more than three thousand Native Americans lived along the woodland rivers of present-day New Hampshire. All of the Native American groups in this area were part of a larger group called the eastern Algonquins. The most prominent Algonquins in New Hampshire were the Abenaki and the Pennacook. They fished and hunted beaver, deer, and moose. They also grew small crops of beans, corn, and squash. Their homes were made out of wood and bark, which they sometimes lined with furs for warmth.

The first Europeans to encounter these Native American groups may have been the Vikings. The Vikings were an aggressive, seafaring people from Scandinavia who attempted to establish colonies in North America around 1000. Some historians believe there is some evidence that they may have landed on the coast of New England, but they did not establish any permanent settlements.

In 1603 English sea captain Martin Pring explored the harbor of the Piscataqua River in the southeastern part of present-day New Hampshire. Two years later the

A statue of Franklin Pierce stands outside New Hampshire's state capitol in Concord. Pierce, who was born in Hillsboro, was President of the United States from 1853 to 1857.

New Hampshire's coastline probably looks much the same as it did in the days of the early European explorers. Today, forests cover about eighty percent of New Hampshire.

French explorer Samuel de Champlain also visited the area. He mapped nearly all of the New England coast, including New Hampshire, Maine, and Massachusetts. He also discovered a group of rocky islands off the coast now called the Isles of Shoals. When Captain John Smith of England came to the same islands in 1614, he named them Smith's Islands. Smith explored the area more thoroughly than Champlain did. He even published a book that described his trip to what is now New England.

Smith's explorations of New England were what first interested England's King James I in the region. The king was eager to send settlers to New England to protect the claims that Smith had made. In 1622 King James signed a land grant that included present-day New Hampshire and part of Maine. He gave the land to John Mason and Sir Ferdinando Gorges, two English merchants. However, the first landowner in the New Hampshire area to start a permanent settlement was David Thomson of Scotland. In 1623 Thomson began a settlement south of today's town of Portsmouth and named it Pannaway Plantation. Another settlement was founded about this time by Edward and William Hilton. Their settlement later grew into the town of Dover.

In 1629 Mason and Gorges divided their land. Gorges called his share Maine, and John Mason called his share New Hampshire. By 1640 New Hampshire had two more towns, Exeter and Hampton, making a total of four. The population of the four towns together was barely one thousand. The towns had trouble forming a unified government, so in 1641 they decided to submit to the rule of the Massachusetts Bay Colony.

By this time the New Hampshire settlers had begun trading fish and furs with the Abenaki. The Abenaki also taught the settlers the best methods for farming and hunting. The Abenaki were becoming increasingly angry with the settlers, however. The settlers were clearing the forests to build settlements and farms. They also started trading lumber for goods overseas. Animals that the Abenaki hunted began to move farther west as more trees were cut down. The shipbuilding industry began in New Hampshire about this time.

The settler population was just under three thousand when King Charles II declared the New Hampshire

above. Captain John Smith was one of the first explorers of the New Hampshire coast. In 1620 the Pilgrims used Smith's book about the area, *A Description of New England*, to find their way to their settlement in Massachusetts.

below. This drawing depicts Sir Ferdinando Gorges and John Mason naming their provinces.

area a separate royal province in 1679. But the English weren't the only ones settling in present-day New Hampshire and the rest of North America. Many French trappers and traders believed that they had as much right to use the land as the English did. Disputes between France and Great Britain over the land and control of the area's trading led to a conflict between the two countries in 1754 that came to be called the French and Indian War. Both the French and the British gained the help of Native Americans during the war. The French had more Native American allies, however, because the two groups had always maintained a relatively peaceful trading relationship. In 1763 the war ended when the British and French signed the Treaty of Paris. The treaty awarded most of North America east of the Mississippi to the British. The remaining Abenaki, Pennacook, and other Algonquin groups were forced to leave their homeland and resettle in Canada.

The French and Indian War cost Great Britain a lot of money. The British government felt it was fair to raise the colonists' taxes to help pay the cost of driving off the French. The British also added new taxes to goods that had never been taxed before, such as news-papers and documents. The colonists became angry, especially because Great Britain imposed these taxes without allowing the colonists to voice their opinion on the matter. Talk of starting a revolution against Great Britain swept through the colonies.

New Hampshire residents were some of the first colonists to turn that talk into action. On December

14, 1774, a group of about four hundred armed New Hampshire colonists attacked Fort William and Mary, near Portsmouth. They captured weapons and ammunition that would soon be used to mount a full-scale revolution.

The Revolutionary War began in Massachusetts in April 1775. Colonists forced New Hampshire's royal governor out of the area two months later. Although no battles were fought on New Hampshire soil, New Hampshire volunteers were in many battles. Large portions of forestland were cut down to supply wood for warships, which was the beginning of New Hampshire's shipbuilding industry. New Hampshire was the first state to start an independent colonial government when it adopted a state constitution in January 1776.

The Revolutionary War continued until 1783. In 1788 New Hampshire's ratification of the United States Constitution was the deciding vote that put the Constitution into effect. About 140,000 settlers lived in New Hampshire at this time. Most of them were farmers. In fact, by the first part of the 1800s, agriculture was New Hampshire's most important economic activity. Shipbuilding also continued to thrive after the war. A few settlers also continued to make their living from fishing and fur trading.

New industries began to spring up in New Hampshire. The state's first cotton textile mill opened in 1804. By the 1850s factories in New Hampshire

Pictured here is the *Ranger,* a Revolutionary War ship built at New Hampshire's Portsmouth shipyards. It was the first ship to fly the Stars and Stripes flag of the United States.

produced cloth, shoes, machinery, and paper and wood products. Most of these factories were water-powered, and dams were built on rivers throughout the state. New Hampshire's residents moved to cities to work at these factories, and mill towns, such as Manchester, expanded rapidly. Although the economy of New Hampshire and the rest of the new nation was thriving, other problems arose.

Disagreements sprang up between the northern and southern states over trade, states' rights, and especially slavery. While African slaves were used extensively by southern plantation owners, slavery had disappeared from the northern states by the 1820s. Many northerners found slavery immoral and thought that the South should outlaw it, too. In 1861 the arguments led to the Civil War between the Union in the North and the Confederacy in the South.

New Hampshire's shipyards again produced warships, this time for the Union's fight to bring the Confederate states back into the Union. The Union Army wore uniforms made from New Hampshire textiles and shoes made from New Hampshire leather. About five thousand New Hampshire soldiers gave their lives for the Union victory by the end of the Civil War in 1865.

New Hampshire's industries continued to thrive after the Civil War, and the state gained a reputa-

This drawing shows a nineteenth-century factory in New Hampshire. Manufacturing first began to overtake agriculture in importance to the state during the Civil War.

tion for being industrial as well as agricultural. By the mid-1870s factories employed well over fifty percent of the state's workers. Many farmers left New Hampshire as manufacturing began to take over the economy. In fact, the population actually decreased between 1860 and 1870. But the population grew again as immigrants moved to New Hampshire and found jobs in the factories. Around 1890, tourists began to come to New Hampshire for breathtaking views and fresh air. Resorts were built to accommodate the new tourist industry.

At the turn of the century, New Hampshire's population was well over four hundred thousand. Factories continued to thrive, but poor working conditions gave them a bad reputation. Many owners of shoe and textile factories took advantage of their workers, of which many were women and children. The factory owners forced them to work long hours under dangerous conditions for little pay. In the early 1900s, state legislators passed laws to limit working hours and to institute safety inspections.

The state legislature also passed laws to protect the land. Logging and woodworking industries had stripped much of the state's forests. People in New

Before becoming President, Franklin Pierce served as a Brigadier General in the Mexican War.

Hampshire began to realize that no trees at all would be left if the logging industry continued at that pace. Citizens formed the Society for the Protection of New Hampshire Forests. In 1911 the state persuaded the federal government to protect a large section of the White Mountain forests.

The United States entered World War I in 1917, and New Hampshire's factories again began production of war materials. The state's workers manufactured uniforms, shoes, and ships—including some of the nation's first successful submarines. Over twenty thousand of the American soldiers who served in World War I were from New Hampshire.

By the 1920s Manchester's Amoskeag textile mills were the largest in the world. The textile industry had reached its peak, however. Production slowed in New Hampshire as new textile factories opened in the South. In the 1930s the Great Depression hit the entire nation. Banks and factories closed, and millions of people across the nation lost their jobs. About one in every five people in New Hampshire was out of work in the early 1930s. To make matters worse, the state was struck by a severe flood in 1936 and a hurricane in 1938. The damage from the two added up to almost sixty million dollars.

Industry in the state was salvaged when the United States entered World War II in 1941. About sixty thousand New Hampshire residents served as soldiers in the war. About twenty thousand more served by working in the factories that made weapons and ships, including submarines. Agriculture also experienced growth as more and more food was needed to feed the soldiers overseas.

In July 1944, just before the end of World War II, New Hampshire was the site of an important event in world history. Governmental representatives of 44 countries met at Bretton Woods. Delegates conferring amidst the peaceful beauty of New Hampshire's White Mountains planned two agencies that help to maintain the world's economy—the World Bank and the International Monetary Fund.

When World War II ended in 1945, the government of New Hampshire worked to avoid letting a postwar slowdown in factory production ruin the state's economy. The state began to recruit new companies that manufactured electronic products such as televisions and, later, computers. New Hampshire's tourism industry also began to advertise more aggressively. Both winter and summer tourists flocked to the state, especially for the seclusion and the ski resorts of

Secretary of the Treasury, Henry Morgenthau, Jr., speaks at the opening meeting of the Bretton Woods Monetary Conference on July 2, 1944. Delegates at the conference planned the future of world trade.

the White Mountains.

In May 1961 New Hampshire proudly sent one of its residents on one of the most exciting missions in American history. Alan Shepard, born in East Derry, became the first American in space when he briefly orbited the earth in a rocket. Tragedy prevented New Hampshire from sending its second resident into space 25 years later. Concord's Christa McAuliffe, who would have been the first civilian in space, died when the space shuttle *Challenger* exploded just after liftoff in January 1986.

Many New Hampshire residents consider another recent event, the 1990 opening of the Seabrook nuclear power plant, a tragedy of a different sort.
Since 1973 environmental activists have fought against construction of the plant. They believe that nuclear reactors are unsafe because of the danger of radiation leaking into the environment. Yet the Seabrook nuclear power plant has greatly reduced New Hampshire's

East Derry resident Alan Shepard gained national fame in 1961 as the first American in space in the space capsule *Freedom 7*. He later commanded the third mission to the moon in *Apollo 14*.

Two girls are arrested at the Seabrook Station nuclear power plant in March 1990. The girls sat down and blocked the entrance to the plant in protest when it was licensed for operation.

dependency on oil- and coal-fired generating plants for electricity. Many citizens, however, believe that the environmental price in the long run may be too high.

The 1990s brought New Hampshire into the spotlight for many more positive reasons. New Hampshire has repeatedly been voted one of the best places to live in the nation. In addition, the state's Business and Finance Authority has continued to attract new industry to the state. The practical people of New Hampshire have done more than keep pace with the modern era. In many respects they've gone beyond it.

Reaching for the Stars

Christa McAuliffe always thought of herself as an "ordinary person." But there must have been something extraordinary about her. Out of more than 11,000 people who applied to be the first teacher in space, NASA chose Christa McAuliffe. For her it also meant something more. "When I was young, women did not fly in space," she explained.

Why would a 37-year-old high school teacher with a normal life in Concord, New Hampshire, take such a risk? Maybe because she loved to teach. She wanted to teach children about space—not just from photographs and telescopes, but from personal experience. Christa planned to teach two classes from space! When she returned she would have made speeches across the country. She wanted to share the joy of space travel with everyone. "I would like . . . to bring back the wonder of it all," she said.

Christa McAuliffe probably would have done it, too. And done it well. Her students say she could get everyone involved in class. Even the quiet ones joined in. She shared a part of her life with her students. She made them feel that what they learned would be important in their lives. She helped them want to do their best and work their hardest.

Christa McAuliffe planned to keep a journal of her trip on the Challenger as a way of sharing the experience of space flight with students.

The most advanced planetarium projection system in the world can be found at the Christa McAuliffe Planetarium. It can simulate space travel in three dimensions up to six hundred light years from Earth and a million years into the future or past.

Christa McAuliffe grew up in a housing project in Boston. Even then she liked to explore. Her family remembers that once she set off riding through the busy streets on her tricycle. Her adventure was cut short by the family dog, who ran into the road and circled her tricycle, barking until the cars stopped. "We never did figure out where she was going," her father said. Christa grew up with four younger brothers and sisters. She earned average grades in school. After high school she went to college, got married, and had two children. Christa was active in her community. She loved to learn and loved to teach.

After she was chosen for the shuttle journey, Christa went through some tough training. She enjoyed the training, especially the weightlessness. She said it made her feel like Peter Pan or Superman. Christa had feared she would not do well in training. She'd also been afraid the "real" astronauts would not like her. They did like her, though, and her training went very well.

Christa was not fearful of going into space. Many space shuttles had completed their missions and returned without any problem. By 1986 space travel had become almost routine. The crowd that came to watch the space shuttle *Challenger* take off at Cape Canaveral was happy and excited. Christa's family was there to experience the event. Schoolchildren all over the country were watching on television. Christa and the other astronauts—Francis Scobee, Michael Smith, Ellison Onizuka, Judith Resnik, Ronald McNair, and Gregory Jarvis—smiled and waved as they entered the shuttle. It was the morning of January 28, 1986, and the shuttle lifted off into a cold, blue sky.

Only a minute after liftoff, the shuttle exploded. At first many spectators thought it was just part of the mission—a routine separation of the rocket from the shuttle vehicle. Slowly the unthinkable became a reality. Everyone on board the shuttle was dead.

In June 1990 the Christa McAuliffe Planetarium in Concord, New Hampshire, opened to the public. The planetarium is a theater that

Pictured here are the seven members of the Challenger *crew.*

The space shuttle Challenger *lifts off at Kennedy Space Center. The space-craft had been into space nine times before the disaster, and was considered to be very safe.*

designed the planetarium wanted to make a facility that kept Christa's dream alive—to improve education by giving people experiences they otherwise might never have. The Christa McAuliffe Planetarium has many high-tech controls, sound channels, and special-effects machines. Visitors lean back in special chairs and look at scenes from space. The scenes are projected by computer-controlled projectors with videotapes and laser disks. In this way people can experience space in a special way.

Christa McAuliffe was an ordinary person with a special goal. She wanted people, including herself, to learn more. When she entered the space program, she restated her goal. "What are we doing here?" she said. "We're reaching for the stars."

projects multimedia images of the skies and the stars on a forty-foot domed ceiling. Visitors go into the planetarium to learn about the sky. The people who

A Foundation for a High-Tech Economy

New Hampshire built an economy out of small mills and factories. These factories have remained small, and their role in the state's economy is still very important. All that's changed is the product. Manufacturing accounts for about 23 percent of New Hampshire's economy, employing almost one hundred thousand workers. The state's most important manufactured products are machinery and scientific instruments. Machinery includes everything from computers to aircraft parts. Compaq Computer Corporation in Nashua and Salem is a large computer company that employs thousands of workers. Scientific instruments include airplane control panels, medical equipment, and tools used by weather forecasters.

The fastest-growing area of manufacturing in New Hampshire is electrical and electronic equipment. Lockheed Sanders in Nashua makes electrical components used for military defense. Almost all of these high-tech companies are found in the southeastern part of the state.

Manchester is New Hampshire's largest city and its major industrial center.

A number of high-tech companies are now centered around Boston and in the southern part of Massachusetts. New Hampshire's workers have benefited from this location. A great many people live in New Hampshire and commute to jobs in the greater Boston area. These people find it worth the extra time it takes to travel to and from work. One reason is that New Hampshire's peaceful and beautiful surroundings are becoming harder to find elsewhere.

About 85 percent of New Hampshire's land is still forested. Although much of this forest land is protected, the logging and woodworking industries are still an important part of the state's agricultural income. This is especially true in December, when Christmas trees are in demand.

New Hampshire's most important agricultural product, however, is milk. There are many dairy farms scattered across the state. The main crop in New Hampshire is hay, most of which is used to feed its

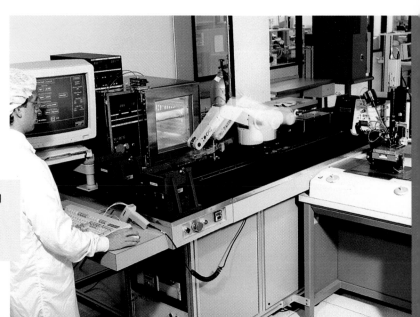

This worker is assembling microwave circuitry at a Lockheed Sanders electronics plant.

dairy and beef cattle. Other agricultural products
produced in the state are eggs, corn, poultry, apples,
and maple syrup. In all, agriculture provides less than
one percent of New Hampshire's income. However, it
is still an important way of life for the families working
the almost three thousand farms in the state.

Mining is a traditional occupation that still plays a
part in New Hampshire's economy. Countless buildings, including the United Nations
in New York City and the Library of
Congress in the nation's capital,
contain granite mined from New
Hampshire's quarries. In addition,
New Hampshire's sand and gravel
have helped build the nation's roads.

By far the fastest-growing area of
New Hampshire's economy is service
industries. Workers in service jobs do
not make products; instead they help

Christmas trees are a small
but important industry in
New Hampshire. Evergreens
make up about two thirds of
the state's forests.

or work for other people. Service employees work in department stores, banks, and repair shops. All together, New Hampshire's service industries now generate over 75 percent of the state's income.

New Hampshire's largest category of service industries is finance, insurance, and real estate. Workers in this area include bank tellers, insurance salespeople, and real estate agents. Liberty Mutual Insurance and Citizen's Bank are two of the state's largest employers in this category.

The next most important category of service industries in New Hampshire is community, social, and personal services. These services employ over 160,000 of New Hampshire's workers, more than any other industry in the state. Doctors, nurses, mechanics, lawyers, and teachers can be listed under this service category. Two of the state's most prominent employers within this category are Elliot Hospital and Dartmouth Hitchcock Medical Center, which is affiliated with Dartmouth College.

Most workers involved with New Hampshire's huge tourist industry are associated with the state's community, social, and personal services. These workers are mostly employed by resorts, hotels, and privately owned tourist attractions. In all, tourists and the tourism industry generate about three billion dollars for the state each year. New Hampshire's annual tourists outnumber its residents by nearly ten to one!

The computer software industry is also helping to expand the number of service jobs in New Hampshire. About ten thousand of New Hampshire's workers were

This photo shows a granite quarry near Concord.

employed by the nearly eight hundred companies in the state in the early 1990s. In addition, the growth in software is continuing, as about half of these companies are planning to expand in the second half of the decade.

New Hampshire is no longer dependent on the textile and shoemaking industries that once were the core of its economic foundation. The buildings that housed these industries are still needed, however. Many new, high-tech corporations have renovated old factories. It seems the right thing to do, considering that these buildings represent the hard and careful work that originally made New Hampshire's economy sturdy.

Spectacular views, such as this one at Franconia Notch, help keep tourism in New Hampshire a three billion-dollar industry.

The Balsams Grand Resort Hotel at Dixville Notch was opened in 1866, when New Hampshire first began to be recognized as a tourist area.

Suffering from Too Much Success

North Conway is a small, scenic town in the Mount Washington Valley. During tourist season, however, North Conway doesn't seem small. The visitors can outnumber the town's residents by ten times or more. Although North Conway benefits from the tourism, the tourists can make life for the town's residents pretty difficult.

"We just went through probably the worst season of all for traffic—the foliage season," said Peter Limmer, a North Conway bootmaker. "All the people come from southern New England up to northern New England to witness the leaves changing. And it's a spectacular time of the year, there's no doubt about it. But the Valley absolutely comes to a standstill because of the crush of people trying to get through."

The traffic problems in North Conway soon became so aggravating that city and state legislators began looking for solutions. But the solution they finally came up with has angered and worried many local residents.

New Hampshire's Department of Transportation is planning a highway bypass to accommodate the growing tourist traffic. But the bypass that they came up with will cut through valuable farmland and wetlands. It also may steer tourists away from North Conway's local shops and hotels. And some residents of North Conway, who have enjoyed the town's peace and beauty for years, and even generations, will have a multilane highway in their backyard.

Frank Hubbell's family has lived on Tasker Hill for four generations. But if

Peter Limmer measures a shoe in his boot shop.

30

A major highway bypass is expected to cut through the campus of Frank Hubbell's wilderness school—passing at one point only one hundred fifty feet behind a newly constructed dorm.

the bypass goes through, Hubbell may have to leave. ". . . it's land that's been in the family generations. It started with my great-grandfather. So we've got roots here. And because of that, we're going to hold out until the last possible minute."

Hubbell and many of North Conway's residents are doing more than just "holding out," however. They've written hundreds of letters to local, state, and federal legislators. They've spoken at town meetings, gathered signatures for petitions, and held protests. But many of them feel that the Department of Transportation just doesn't care.

Growth is forcing people in New Hampshire to make some tough decisions. Some North Conway residents

This covered bridge is the entrance to Jackson, a small town in the White Mountains. Many tourists to New Hampshire visit this part of the state.

feel that legislators need to listen and work with the residents. Otherwise the legislators may not have any North Conway residents left to represent.

31

Inspired by Beauty

The calm and splendor of the New Hampshire landscape has inspired countless artists for hundreds of years. The elegance found in the traditional stone walls, the small towns, and the forests has instilled a distinctively peaceful style in New Hampshire artists.

Perhaps the best known of these New Hampshire artists is the poet Robert Frost. He was born in San Francisco in 1874, and his family moved to New Hampshire when he was 11 years old. Frost made a meager living as a farmer while he pursued his poetry. It took a long time for his work to be appreciated. No American publisher would buy his first book, so he took it to Great Britain, where it was published as *A Boy's Will* in 1913. After the book of poems became successful overseas, his home country took notice. One of his best collections of poetry, published in 1923, is called *New Hampshire*. Visitors tour the Robert Frost Farm in Derry, which is in the southeastern part of the state. This is where Frost lived and worked for more than ten years.

New Hampshire's scenic beauty has inspired artists and craftspeople for centuries.

Robert Frost is one of America's most widely read poets today.

Many people still consider Horace Greeley to be the best newspaper editor of his time.

Novelist John Irving is another important writer from New Hampshire. Born in Exeter in 1942, Irving often uses New Hampshire as the setting for his novels. Irving's best-known novels are *The Hotel New Hampshire* and *The World According to Garp*.

An influential New Hampshire writer from a much earlier period was Horace Greeley. Born in 1811 in Amherst, Greeley became founder and editor of the *New York Tribune* in 1841. Greeley was especially well-known for his antislavery editorials, but he also wrote about many other social issues, including public education and the rights of citizens. He is famous for the phrase, "Go west, young man." These words inspired many men who were struggling to find work in the eastern cities to start a new life in the West.

Another New Hampshire writer and editor was Thomas Bailey Aldrich, born in Portsmouth in 1836. Aldrich spent much of his life working as an editor for the *Atlantic Monthly* magazine, which is still in wide circulation today. Aldrich also became an acclaimed poet and short story writer. First published in 1870, his book *The Story of a Bad Boy* recounts his New Hampshire childhood.

Sarah Josepha Hale, born in Newport in 1788, was one of the country's first female magazine editors. She edited and wrote for a magazine called *Godey's Lady's Book*, which became influential in the lives of nineteenth-century women. She also edited a number of books, including *The Ladies' Wreath*, a collection of poetry by women. Hale also wrote the nursery rhyme "Mary Had a Little Lamb" in 1830.

Another celebrated woman writer from New Hampshire was Mary Baker Eddy. Born near Concord in 1821, Eddy is widely admired for her writing. Her most prominent work is *Science and Health*, which was first published in 1875. In 1908 Eddy founded the *Christian Science Monitor*, a highly acclaimed newspaper that has maintained a wide circulation.

Although Sarah Josepha Hale is best known for her writing and editing, she was also one of the main advocates for making Thanksgiving a national holiday.

New Hampshire women have excelled in many other artistic areas. Painter Elizabeth Gardner Bouguereau, born in Exeter in 1837, was the first American woman to win a gold medal from the exclusive French Academy of Art. Pianist and composer Amy Marcy Beach, born in Henniker in 1867, became a professional pianist by the time she was 16. She went on to write many pieces, including *Gaelic Symphony*, which was the first symphony composed by an American woman.

New Hampshire, the Granite State, supplies much of the stone used for sculptures around the world. The state has raised at least one famous sculptor, Daniel Chester French, born in Exeter in 1850. French is best known for his statues of American heroes. French's first commission, the famous Minute Man statue, was ordered by Concord, Massachusetts, the site of one of the first battles of the Revolutionary War. His most famous sculpture is of Abraham Lincoln in the Lincoln Memorial in our nation's capital.

Sculptor Daniel Chester French completed *The Minute Man*, his first commission, when he was only 23 years old.

There are many artists' "colonies" scattered across the state. These are quiet places where artists can work in peaceful, natural surroundings. One of the most famous New Hampshire artists' colonies was the Cornish Colony. This artist's colony developed around

Lake Winnipesaukee is New Hampshire's largest lake. Many people come here to relax and enjoy the solitude that comes with nature.

the home of the famous sculptor Augustus Saint-Gaudens who moved to the town of Cornish in 1885. This colony has not been used since 1935, but visitors can still tour the area. It was designated as a national historic site in 1965.

Many artists have benefited from working at the MacDowell Colony in Peterborough. Some of the MacDowell Colony's more famous alumni include musicians Leonard Bernstein and Aaron Copland, and writers James Baldwin, Thornton Wilder, and Willa Cather.

The culture of New Hampshire isn't only made up of famous names. Symphonies, ballet and theater companies, and other showcases for local performers thrive throughout the state. Many of these organizations rely on the efforts of the New Hampshire State Council on the Arts.

New Hampshire's scenic beauty has always been one of the state's strong points. New Hampshire's highest mountain, Mount Washington, is the home of the first cog railway to be built in the United States. The railway was completed in 1869. The Old Man of the Mountain, also known as the "Great Stone Face," is a forty-foot high granite formation on Profile Mountain. It is so distinctively New Hampshire that it is the state's official trademark. The best cultural expressions of New Hampshire, whether natural or created by artists, are clearly exceptional.

Autumn colors are one of New Hampshire's main attractions. Foliage festivals are held across the state every year.

Making Your Own Way

Many people dream of becoming their own boss. For artists like Suzanne Lupien and Christopher Gowell, that dream is a reality. Lupien and Gowell support themselves using a combination of hard work and creative thinking.

Suzanne Lupien lives in rural New Hampshire, and she's almost entirely self-sufficient. Her house is heated by wood that she cuts. She fixes her own tools and hauls in her drinking water.

"I love to make something from nothing," Lupien remarks. "I never spend money on materials . . . and a lot of time I see people making nothing out of something. I really like turning that around."

Many people go to the woods to find independence and a sense of freedom. Lupien has found these things in her entire way of life. Lupien paints and sculpts works of art, but she also molds her own life into the form she wants it to take.

"I have so much freedom," says Lupien. "I have the physical freedom of the land and also I'm free to organize my time . . . which may be the reason why I do it."

In urban New Hampshire, sculptor Christopher Gowell is making her own way in the world, too. Gowell is one of New Hampshire's most respected artists.

This 1993 bronze sculpture by Suzanne Lupien is called "Horse and Rider."

Suzanne Lupien (right) clamps a mold in place prior to pouring bronze.

She became a success by marketing her work and convincing other people that her work is important.

"In my studio," Gowell explains, ". . . I reach the natural 'high' of creation. Only to come down hard when I realize I must . . . market my work . . . in a world that often does not value its artists."

Gowell can support herself in the independent life of an artist in part because she is willing to do many different kinds of work. In addition to sculpting and teaching sculpture, Gowell designs toys. She has also drawn cartoons, illustrated books, and designed billboards.

Like Lupien, Gowell enjoys the process of making something from nothing. "Sculpture is . . . a very physical process," says Gowell. When she's sculpting, Gowell pays such close attention that she feels she is "one with the piece in progress."

Gowell usually works with clay, making a mold and then casting the work in bronze. She also has carved in slate, ivory, and soapstone, and is learning silversmithing. Recently, Gowell has begun oil painting.

There are two ways to travel through life—you can either follow in someone else's footsteps or make it up as you go along. As artists, Suzanne Lupien and Christopher Gowell shape their lives in the way they choose. They make it up as they go along.

The French Among the Yankees

In the early 1800s, immigrants from around the world brought their families to America, the "land of opportunity." Eager to fit into their new surroundings, many of these new citizens adopted the English language and American culture as quickly as possible. Many rich cultural traditions were lost for good. Some groups, however, realized the importance of maintaining their culture in an unfamiliar land. In New Hampshire and the rest of New England, one of the most prominent of these groups is the Franco-Americans.

The first Franco-Americans were hunters and trappers who lived in the forests of Quebec in Canada. The first French settlers in North America began arriving at the turn of the seventeenth century. Like our own pioneers, they built farms in the wilderness.

But Quebec was not an easy place to settle. The land was not rich, and the growing season was short. The farms could not provide enough food for so many people. Some of these people resettled in other parts of Canada. In the late 1800s, many others moved south to find factory jobs across the border in New Hampshire and the rest of New England.

Thousands of Canadians, mostly from Quebec, arrived in New England between 1860 and 1930. Most worked long hours in New England shoemaking factories and textile and paper mills. Many others worked as

Father Ray Gagnon is a Roman Catholic priest. The Catholic Church is the center of life in many small Franco-American towns, where services may be conducted in French or English.

lumberjacks, brickmakers, nurses, office workers, and carpenters.

Today, almost one quarter of New Hampshire's residents are Franco-Americans. They're just as proud of their culture today as they were back in the nineteenth century. As Franco-American priest Father Ray Gagnon explains, "No matter where we are, it's important for us to keep that contact. If someone were to come up and say, well, 'I'm a Yankee because I'm from New Hampshire,' I'd be quick to point out that I am not a Yankee. Not because I don't like Yankees. Just because I feel there's a world of difference between us."

The Franco-American spirit has stayed with its people no matter where they are. Franco-Americans have kept their own culture, their own traditions, and their own way of seeing the world. And they're going to try to keep their rich culture alive for many years to come.

St. Anne's Catholic Church, the rich interior of which is shown here, was built in Berlin, New Hampshire, and has a large Franco-American congregation. Catholicism was one of the strongest ties between New Hampshire's Franco-Americans in their new land.

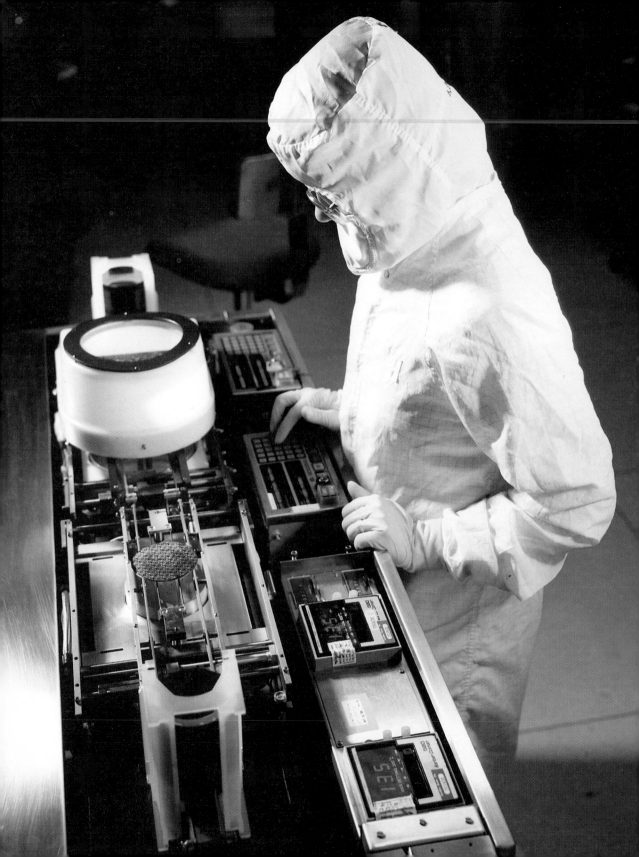

Adding Up the Price of Change

New Hampshire has been a state defined by small towns for almost its entire history. Small towns are still common in New Hampshire. However, they are being threatened by rapid population and business expansion. As businesses and people move into a small town, the character of the town changes. The town loses the peace that comes with living close to natural surroundings. New Hampshire's consistently high ratings in business magazines have attracted corporations and boosted the state's economy. The population has grown by over twenty percent since 1980. This rapid expansion has put New Hampshire's historic small towns at risk.

In the early 1990s, concerned citizens worked to pass laws that would keep home and business expansion from moving onto untouched land. These laws have succeeded in protecting about one hundred thousand acres from development. More steps such as these will likely be needed in the future to balance expansion and nature.

Computer and electrical equipment production in New Hampshire has increased in recent years and will be a major industry in the state's future.

New Hampshire's peaceful solitude is being threatened by booming business development and rapid population increases.

The state has a long list of recent accomplishments that spell good news for the future. Perhaps the most important of these is that the state's high school students have the highest graduation rate in New England. In addition, New Hampshire businesses work closely with the state's colleges, helping to keep over eighty percent of technical college graduates in the state's workforce. This emphasis on education ensures that New Hampshire will always have a skilled and competitive workforce.

The people of New Hampshire do not resist change for its own sake. They merely want to hold on to what is good about the state and good for the state.

Important Historical Events

1000 The Vikings may have explored the coast of New Hampshire around this time.

1603 Martin Pring explores the mouth of the Piscataqua River.

1605 The French explorer Samuel de Champlain explores and maps nearly all of the New England coast.

1614 English Captain John Smith explores and maps New England.

1622 The Council of New England grants land to English merchants John Mason and Sir Ferdinando Gorges.

1623 David Thomson of Scotland starts a settlement in New Hampshire at Pannaway Plantation.

1629 Mason and Gorges divide their land grant. John Mason names his share New Hampshire.

1641 New Hampshire becomes part of the Massachusetts Bay Colony.

1679 Charles II makes New Hampshire a separate royal province. The population has reached about three thousand.

1763 The Treaty of Paris ends the French and Indian War.

1774 New Hampshire colonists seize weapons and ammunition from Fort William and Mary, near Portsmouth.

1775 The Revolutionary War begins in April. New Hampshire colonists force their royal governor out of the state in June.

1776 In January New Hampshire becomes the first state to adopt its own constitution.

1783 The Revolutionary War ends.

1784 New Hampshire adopts its current state constitution.

1788 New Hampshire becomes the ninth and deciding state to ratify the Constitution of the United States.

1803 New Hampshire's first cotton textile mill opens.

1838 The first New Hampshire railroad starts running.

1853 Franklin Pierce from New Hampshire becomes the fourteenth President of the United States.

1885 Robert Frost moves to New Hampshire at age eleven.

1918 White Mountain National Forest is established.

1936 New Hampshire is struck by a severe flood.

1938 New Hampshire and other New England states are struck by a hurricane.

1944 The World Bank and the International Monetary Fund are created during a conference held in New Hampshire's Bretton Woods.

1961 Alan Shepard, a native of New Hampshire, becomes the first American in space.

1973 New Hampshire residents begin their fight against the proposed Seabrook nuclear power plant.

1986 Concord resident Christa McAuliffe and six astronauts are killed when the space shuttle *Challenger* explodes in January.

1990 The Seabrook nuclear power plant is opened, despite much popular protest.

1992 New Hampshire creates a state Business and Finance Authority to attract new industry.

New Hampshire's flag depicts the state seal, encircled by nine stars and yellow laurel leaves, on a blue background. The nine stars represent that New Hampshire was the ninth state to enter the Union. The ship depicted on the state seal is the *Raleigh,* which was built in Portsmouth for the Revolutionary War.

New Hampshire Almanac

Nickname. The Granite State

Capital. Concord

State Bird. Purple finch

State Flower. Purple lilac

State Tree. White birch

State Motto. Live Free or Die

State Song. "Old New Hampshire"

State Abbreviations. N.H. (traditional); NH (postal)

Statehood. June 21, 1788, the 9th state

Government. Congress: U.S. senators, 2; U.S. representatives, 2. State Legislature: senators, 24; representatives, 400. Counties: 10

Area. 9,283 sq mi (24,044 sq km), 44th in size among the states

Greatest Distances. north/south, 180 mi (289 km); east/west, 93 mi (150 km). Coastline: 13 mi (21 km)

Elevation. Highest: Mount Washington, 6,288 ft (1,917 m). Lowest: sea level, along the Atlantic Ocean

Population. 1990 Census: 1,113,915 (21% increase over 1980), 41st among the states. Density: 120 persons per sq mi (46 persons per sq km). Distribution: 51% urban, 49% rural. 1980 Census: 920,610

Economy. *Agriculture*: milk, timber and Christmas trees, hay, apples, eggs, corn, poultry, maple syrup. *Manufacturing*: machinery, scientific instruments, electrical and electronic equipment. *Mining*: granite, sand and gravel

State Seal

State Bird: Purple finch

State Flower: Purple lilac

Annual Events

★ World Championship Sled Dog Races in Laconia (February)

★ Wildquack River Festival in Jackson (May)

★ International Children's Festival in Somersworth (June)

★ Revolutionary War Days Festival in Exeter (July)

★ Monadnock Balloon and Aviation Festival in Keene (August)

★ League of New Hampshire Craftsmen's Fair in Sunapee (August)

★ World Mud Bowl in North Conway (September)

★ Sandwich Fair in Center Sandwich (October)

★ Christmas in New England in Portsmouth (December)

Places to Visit

★ Annalee Doll Museum in Meredith

★ Cathedral of the Pines in Rindge

★ Christa McAuliffe Planetarium in Concord

★ Conway Scenic Railroad in North Conway

★ Daniel Webster's birthplace, near Franklin

★ Heritage New Hampshire in Glen

★ Mount Washington Cog Railway, near Bretton Woods

★ Museum of New Hampshire History in Concord

★ Old Man of the Mountain and Flume Gorge, at Franconia Notch

★ Robert Frost Farm, near Derry

★ White Mountain National Forest in north-central New Hampshire